To TV

C000070856

V

Worcester's
Media Mile

best wishes,

A walking guide to TV locations
and other memorable media milestones
around the city

Mike Jackson

Mike Jackson

SPLASH TV

First published 2021

ISBN: 9798713063085

This modest publication provides a paper record of Mike Jackson's popular guided walks through Worcester. If you have done one, then here's the data that determined the route.

If you have not taken a stroll with Mike, then this might make such an outing unnecessary - or could encourage you to hear the tales from the ex-TV producer's mouth at first hand. Mike worked for the broadcasters and his own video production company for many years in this part of the world.

Many people have been greatly amused by his revelations of crises, dramas and mishaps behind the scenes. We hope you will be too.

Contents

Pages 4 & 5 offer a simplified guide to the route, indicating the location of each text Scene, starting with The Guildhall on Page 6.

Intermittently, readers will find reflections without a geographic hook. The Index at the back of the book, starting on Page 95, will direct you to the relevant anecdote or incident.

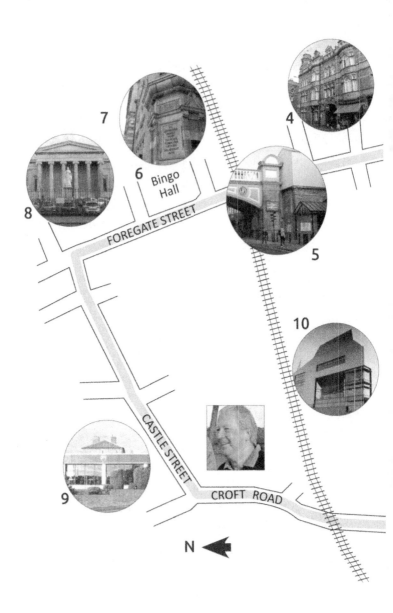

7

6 Bingo Hall

4

8

FOREGATE STREET

5

10

CASTLE STREET

9

CROFT ROAD

N

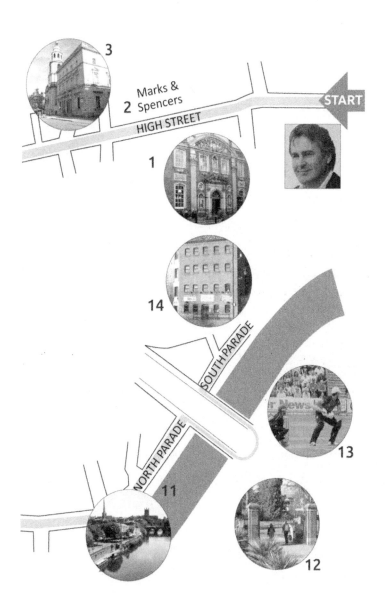

3

Marks &
2 Spencers

START

HIGH STREET

1

14

SOUTH PARADE

NORTH PARADE

11

13

12

Scene 1 Guildhall

What a fine building. How lucky we are it is still standing and continuing to enjoy functional status in our marvellous city. As a citizen I have entered the premises many times. As a TV producer, I went in with cameras on three occasions. Firstly, as an 'Antiques Roadshow' director in 1999 to film our very own Henry Sandon examining porcelain treasures in the Mayor's Parlour for a sequence for the programme opening.

My second visit was in 2009 when I persuaded the then Mayor, Councillor Mrs Lucy Hodgson, to allow me to make a "video diary" of a typical week of her mayoralty. The previous year I had co-ordinated video projects for the BBC's trial run of Local TV in Herefordshire, and had spent an amusing day with Marcelle Lloyd-Hayes as Mayor of Hereford to make a short film for that short-lived TV service.

I reckoned there was more material in this vein that could be acquired in Worcester – bigger city; more happening. It turned out that Lucy Hodgson and I were ex-colleagues. I had worked as a director at Pebble Mill in Birmingham when she was in charge of the catering there – a huge operation, providing midday hot lunches for hundreds of TV folk in a vast canteen on the top floor of that vibrant building in Edgbaston.

Mrs Hodgson was understandably wary of having a camera follow her around; not to mention having a radio microphone pinned to her clothes so I could capture everything she said as it happened. We agreed that she would have the final say as to what the finished film included, or, of course, left out.

And so began a fascinating week – me with camera trying to be a "fly-on-the-wall" where possible, but also, as necessary, asking Mrs Hodgson and her associates to make changes to their movements in order to acquire appealing shots (this is directing good practice – avoiding ugly backgrounds, low light areas, nasty shadows or noises off. Sometimes the camera person needs to move somewhere else; other times the subject must be manoeuvred to a slightly different location, or be asked to come through a door again so you can have an image of them passing that threshold from both sides which can be cut together in the edit).

First public engagement was a visit to the highly respected breast cancer unit at the Royal Hospital. We then saw her presenting certificates at various events; opening a school trail (Mayor on knees to be at kids' height for cutting ribbon); and launching a new accommodation block at the University (Mayor in wellies, holding spade of soil close to camera, Vice Chancellor at her shoulder), in between delicious VIP tea parties in the Parlour.

Mrs H's term of office was marked by her capacity to rustle up lovely cakes and buns for her many official visitors. One day I persuaded her to let me film in her home kitchen to watch her bake as she candidly reflected on her responsibilities.

In that week, the Council applied its decision that - for financial reasons - it would no longer support a limo and chauffeur for the city, and so Mrs H had to walk, or drive herself, to some engagements; me in the front passenger seat, swinging the camera between the driver and the road ahead. We titled the film 'Pomp and Circumstance'. My thanks again to Lucy Hodgson for so generously allowing me to capture and present an admirable week of hard toil by a committed public servant.

Third video visit to the Guildhall was as a director on 'Flog It'. The Sunday valuation day started with Paul Martin doing his stylish opening pieces-to-camera on the High Street. This was a good location because no cars could pass. Paul always attracts big crowds of fans wherever he goes. If we were working at the side of a busy road, cars would swerve on to the pavement so the driver or passengers could try to snatch a selfie with the star. I was always fearful of a road accident, and, technically, whatever the cause, it would be concluded in court to have been the director's fault.

Paul is a great cornerstone for the format show, always charming to everyone. People waited for hours to have their precious item evaluated by an off-screen expert who might then recommend the object be featured in front of the cameras. I would then meet the participant, and on more than one occasion I quietly pointed out to the owner that they would soon no longer own that family heirloom – for the dubious reward of maybe £50 and being on day-time TV for a few minutes. Some took my advice.

I had spent many engaging months helping Paul draft his book, 'Paul Martin's Britain' in which he outlines his life and career, explains the mechanics of making hundreds of editions of 'Flog It', and reveals some of his favourite places across the country. Within Worcestershire, Paul documented his enthusiasm for the Malvern Hills and his huge respect for the artist who so superbly and distinctively captured that wonderful landscape, David Prentice.

We had a fruitful day on the ground floor of the Guildhall. Paul had done all his necessary bits by 3 o'clock, so I released him to head home to Wiltshire. We were due to finish at 5.00 pm, and by 4.30 the camera crews had filmed all the chosen item interviews, so I told them they could begin to pack away their kits. At this point a tall, scruffy guy aged about 30 entered the Guildhall. He carried a plastic bag in one hand and pulled a child with the other. As soon as he saw the cameras being dismounted he became agitated. I asked what was wrong. Why were the cameras not operating when no-one had yet seen what was in his bag? I told him he was too late, but we would have an expert look at his belongings. He took umbrage at this. So I suggested he attend the next Flog It valuation day which was being held in Nottingham in a few weeks' time. Now he became extremely angry. I struggled to calm him down. Thankfully a couple of strapping cameramen came and stood alongside me. He was out-numbered and stormed off. Hence no nasty scene to be reported in the Worcester News next day.

Scene 2   Marks & Spencers

Their food products are special – a class above run-of-the-mill supermarket offerings. Or so we thought until 'The Really Useful Show' team turned up to do a taste test on the High Street. I was the director with responsibility for these filmed inserts. We had visited many towns and cities across England offerings a selection of items to passers-by to assess which they found most appealing.

Coming up to Christmas was a perfect time to compare branded Christmas cakes. On our stall we had an example from Tesco, Morrisons, the Co-op and M&S. Participants could not see which brand they were tasting. They could have a nibble at four small slices of cake marked A, B, C and D. Each person had to decide which was the best, and we repeated this exercise with about 40 folk.

A crowd gathered wanting to see how the voting went. Morrisons's version achieved least points, next came Tesco. In second place was M&S, thus putting the Co-op at the top of the table. This produced a mass gasp from the people outside the store, which we had to edit very carefully in order to not be accused of unjustifiably demoting a fine retail business.

I filmed one RUS insert with co-operation from a Tesco store in Warrington. It was the early days of home shopping. This option was available only to those unable to comfortably push round a trolley and take home a bunch of carrier bags. Our researcher had found a disabled ex-army man – a bomb disposal expert who had been blown up by a weapon in Belfast. He was lucky to be alive, but was now wheel-chair-bound. We saw him move through the Tesco branch explaining to an assistant what he required, then we filmed the van arrive at his house for his shopping to be carried to his kitchen table. We never imagined such a service would grow and grow, and eventually become a vital aid to survival through the Covid epidemic lock-downs.

A pre-cursor to 'The One Show', the daily weekday morning Really Useful Show saw two hosts presenting live material from Pebble Mill studios, interspersed with pre-recorded films or live OB - outside broadcast - inserts. One of my least happy experiences was as producer of a Really Useful Show seaside special across four July mornings from the front at Weymouth.

As it was the height of summer, a senior executive decided there was no need for any studio-based elements. Everything would be broadcast live from the holiday location. Intentions were admirable – beach games, sun tan lotion tests, swimwear fashion etc., but we were painfully unprepared for four days of heavy rain which forced us to abandon the beach and huddle in shelters along the prom. Wet and weary, we eventually took cover in a damp café into which star guest Max Bygraves was delivered - sadly not in the best of health.

Several location microphones now broke down from rain-water intrusion and so we had no alternative but to lurch towards the end of the live programme by asking endless questions of the elderly entertainer perched awkwardly on a plastic chair as a hurricane buffeted past outside.

Any viewers who stayed with this surely wondered why the producer had been so keen to learn so much of Max's opinions on car maintenance, washing-up liquids, even funeral services at this point in a once-glittering career. I think both Max and I felt we had died that horrible morning.

Amongst my happiest Really Useful Show outings was an exploration of Worcester's High Street in the delightful company of the always buoyant Irishman John Daly when he celebrated the look and feel of the High Street as an exceptionally pleasing place to shop.

John is now Producer of 'Lightning', the great new BBC2 teatime quiz show presented by Zoe Lyons and staged in Belfast.

Scene 3   The Cross

I spent two years commuting from Worcestershire to Bristol on an almost daily basis – up and down the M5. At dawn and dusk I would roar past all sorts of buildings and structures both sides of the carriageway and wonder what they were. When my Antiques Roadshow directing contract came to an end I decided to explore the hinterland of the artery further. This eventually turned into a book – the M5 Sights Guide.

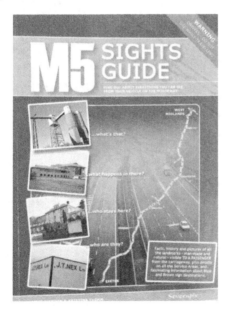

I had researched and photographed the buildings and Kristina Thimm designed a great format forcing the carriageway into a straight line down the middle of each page. The book achieved lots of media exposure and proved very popular.

An important outlet for the book was Waterstones in Worcester. Staff were determined to give this local product a good profile within its fine shop on the High Street just a few doors south of the Guildhall.

Until this crazy project I had not realized the main Birmingham-Bristol trunk road, the A38, originally lay along Worcester's handsome High Street, across The Cross, then right past the Guildhall and the Cathedral.

What a mercy that the motorway took such pressure off our fabulous city.

Call that a Bargain

The BBC's 'Bargain Hunt' is built around a bizarre concept for a game show. The fundamental principle is that competitors buy items at antiques fairs then sell them in auction to hopefully make a profit. But it is generally from auctions that the fair dealers bought those pieces in the first place. Hence the likelihood of profit is low, and thus the result of each game is often that one team has lost less money than the other. Yet over one thousand editions of the programme have been made and new shows or repeats are regularly screened, all achieving good audience figures. Why? What is the magic ingredient?

Essentially viewers like to follow the endeavours and decisions of the participants, learn a little about old objects, and witness the excitement in auction rooms as bidding sends the value of old stuff in unexpected directions.

It's a format show, and the format is sound; the parts assembled with great efficiency and skill by a smart team. Antiques fairs are generally staged across a weekend. If the Bargain Hunt gang are permitted to attend a Fair they will make the front end of four programmes at that location – sixteen competitors will arrive, four each morning, another four each afternoon.

So twice a day the presenter will meet two new blue and red competitors, then separate camera crews will capture the buying process of each couple. A few weeks later everyone attends the same auction where the competitors' purchases are slotted into the sale at intervals of about five items. This is the hairy bit. The presenter and crew have just a few minutes to position and introduce each competitor and their specific items before they go under the hammer. Each time the hammer goes down, those in front of the camera have to deliver a swift and correct reaction to those events and figures, before the next couple are nudged into place for their evaluation and response scenes. All eight couples and their twenty-four items have to be pleasingly and correctly captured across a few hours. Clever, but taxing.

Tim Wonnacott was a Director at Sothebys with special responsibility for miscellaneous items. His knowledge is superb. Some dusty object on the corner of a stall would prove to be of huge historical significance. And Tim could deliver a delightful brief lecture to camera on whatever he had picked up. Time and again I was in awe at his comprehension and eloquence.

A series of episodes were experimentally made without allowing the camera crews to re-stage and re-shoot the "shopping" incidents at a fair. This resulted in far too much footage of participants with their backs to the cameras. I spent months in edit suites devising commentary to be recorded by Tim to give some sense to what had happened on and around those busy tables of old stuff.

Scene 4   Hopmarket

For many years my wife Gil and I lived in the village of Suckley eight miles west of Worcester off the A44. Seventy years ago the village was home to a pioneering manufacturing plant - The Bruff. This firm made clever hop-picking machines that were sold all over the world.

In 2006 I discovered that one of the original machines was still operating in Bishops Frome a few miles away and so made a film of the picking and processing season - which proved an engaging element of the following year's Herefordshire Borderlines Film Festival.

Hops are still grown in the area – not least by the dedicated Capper family at Stocks Farm in Suckley – and originally those sacks or "pockets" of hops would have come for evaluation and sale within the courtyard of this fine brick and tile-decorated building that came into being right at the start of the 20th century.

.

Sounds dodgy

Round the corner from the Hopmarket, as you will know - possibly from the excellent guided history tours enriching the city - Elgar used to play the organ at the Catholic church off Sansome Street.

Until recently the BBC mounted a great musical extravaganza across one weekend of each year – 'Music Live'. This necessitated considerable challenges for musicians and directors. For the latter, it meant effective decisions regarding staging concerts, then getting live sound and pictures bounced up to a satellite for dispersal across the nation's TV transmitters. One year I was assigned a dawn concert from Bristol to be performed in front of a ballet of hot air balloons, after which I was required to deliver a lunchtime steel band gig from the centre of Salisbury. What could go wrong?

A storm through the night meant the balloons could not be launched, and so instead of glorious giant shapes floating above the band, we had the roars and flames of the burners on each balloon basket in the background - turning tranquility into a war zone. Then a hairy drive to Salisbury to discover the advance party had erected the stage in the wrong place and the outside broadcast truck could not beam up a signal from this location to the satellite. With less than an hour before our transmission slot I demanded the staging and truck be moved to the correct sites. I then suffered a long series of angry phone conversations with broadcast engineers in London demanding to know exactly what they would see and hear at noon. A few minutes to twelve, we were up and running. The show itself was relatively easy to handle compared with the previous twelve hours.

At the other end of my musical scale, I made a film for a Welsh local authority to promote its arts provision. This included a visit to an impressive new centre in Caernarfon. After interviewing the manager I began to gather illustrative shots of the interior. In a small music studio a teenage girl was practicing the harp. I asked permission to enter the room and film a few minutes. Her tutor agreed, so I set up my camera and pointed it at the strings as the girl's fingers plucked a lovely Welsh tune. I had never been close to a harp in my life.

The girl could play very well. The beauty of the moment overwhelmed me. I started to weep and had to excuse myself and move on. Yes, distinctly unprofessional.

Scene 5 Foregate Street

This is the busiest railway station in Worcestershire even though it has no car parking. I learnt much about the station and the route to and from Oxford while making a film to mark forty years of lobbying by a determined group of rail travellers who resisted plans to close the line in the early 1970s. British Rail intended to rip up sections of the track and instead operate bus services. The Cotswold Line Promotion Group fought to keep the track and its stations and - essentially - succeeded.

The DVD producing committee were keen I embrace every station on the line, but their budget did not really allow for lengthy visits to every stop. Almost all projects eventually reveal unexpected extra costs that no-one in advance anticipated or warned you about. In this case a new network timetable had serious teething troubles, meaning most trains were travelling later than scheduled or not at all. I wasted hours on country lanes or in farmers' fields pointing the camera at a stretch of track that ought to have had a train zip along it at a certain time – but nothing turned up.

Trying to satisfy the wishes of the Group I arrived at a small halt not far north of Oxford on a wet Sunday afternoon. The single, short platform was only two metres wide. I set the camera up at the front edge to capture a dramatic angle of a passing-through High Speed Train, carefully holding my umbrella over the instrument. I started filming the empty line and continued to record until ten minutes beyond the scheduled time of passing, then gave up. I dismounted the camera and carried my wet gear back down the ramp towards my car. At this moment the HST roared through (at what I was later told would have been close to 100 mph). Thank goodness I had not waited any longer on the platform. I'm sure the train would have swept me and my kit right off on to the rails.

For efficiency, I later made a smart move – at midday on 21st June 2018 - to board one of the High Speed Trains at Evesham, then fully open the vestibule window and point the camera out and so capture angles from the train as it travelled forwards all the way to Hereford and back. Mid-summer day with the sun overhead gave me the Malvern Hills from both sides with minimum shadow - great footage acquired in just a few hours to be deployed at various points in the rail narrative at the mere cost of a stiff neck, ear-ache and a dirty face.

Clips of some of the programmes and films Mike refers to can be found on YouTube. Search: Worcester Media Mile

Ugly scenes

Despite the odd mishap, most of the projects I have worked on have been a memorable privilege. But not universally so. I was once required to direct some episodes of a very poor factual series about room re-decoration. This topic had worked immensely well in peak-time with people such as Alan Titchmarsh enjoying a key anchor role. A channel executive had now seen fit to apply the notion to day-time TV with a small budget and insufficient piloting. The on-screen "experts" had limited abilities, and there were no off-screen experts to back them up; aid them forward.

A house in the suburbs (several not a million miles from here) would be chosen to have a room make-over across two days. The owners would stay in a hotel overnight and return the second afternoon. So essentially the team had one afternoon and evening plus the following morning to transform a kitchen, bedroom or living room. One "expert" concentrated on low cost décor, the other on low cost furniture and fittings. Hence the camera crew hopped between Ms. A messing about with, say, paper flowers and glue, and Mr. B sawing up sheets of MDF (spraying its toxic dust all over the house in the process). Neither was good at explaining what they were trying to achieve, and this was often matched by their inability to produce something satisfactory, never mind pleasing.

But here is the curious thing: when the owners returned and were shown on camera the results of this ropey make-over, the couple – whilst the camera was recording – always performed as you would wish in an ideal world. They gushed over what had been done and indicated their delight at the results. They were often looking at unfinished walls, flaky fireplace surrounds or clumsily built-in wardrobes, but they dutifully sustained the fiction. Then, as soon as we had acquired that key "reveal" scene and turned off the camera, the couple would announce that they did not like what had been done and wanted it put back or done better.

Our experts would now retire to the nearest pub leaving the rest of the team to try to remedy the shortcomings while the camera-person acquired angles of the room that looked okay and could be edited into the "reveal" sequence. At midnight we could still be hoovering MDF dust from all surfaces in children's bedrooms. Shameful. I complained.

Inevitably, sometimes complaints were made against Splash TV and its director, sometimes justified. A firm supplying sophisticated machines for export needed DVD training videos in the box. My first effort was staged in a noisy corner of their factory. I told them that next time it would be better to have a quiet, tidy space. They then called me in for an urgent job on a new prototype and rushed me and my camera into a store room with walls crissed-crossed by ugly wooden batons. In desperation I dashed to a drapery store and bought 16 metres of curtain material to create a bland background, and made the DVD that day. When I added the price of the material to my invoice, they complained that this cost had never been authorised. However, without an ugly scene, the matter was eventually resolved.

Scene 6   Bingo Hall

This place was once a music venue. Biggest draw? The Rolling Stones. My professional inter-action with rock'n'roll has been modest and marginal. But I did meet a Beatle – Ringo Starr – when he was launching the 'Thomas the Tank Engine' series on Children's ITV. He brought to our studio his stunning "Bond-girl" wife Barbara Bach and the somewhat stunned author, Reverend W. Awdry - who had just learned how much money the show's worldwide merchandising would deliver.

I interviewed a 'Blues Brother' in Hollywood –
Dan Aykroyd, while making a film about 'The
Ghostbusters' for Columbia Pictures and ITV.
Dan told us he considered the Slimer ghost
character was a representation of his old buddy
John Belushi.

I narrowly avoided an embarrassing scene with an embryonic pop star at Central Studios in Birmingham. An actress had just left 'Neighbours' and was launching her first single in the UK. I had never heard of her, but next to my office was an open plan area where Children's ITV researchers and guests mingled. I walked in and saw a girl with an Aussie accent on the phone. Fifteen minutes later she was still blathering away. I asked a researcher who this was. "Kylie – talking to her Mum." "Where's the Mum?" "In Australia." "Get her off that phone. I'm not paying for her domestic calls from my budget." Yes, Ms Minogue, before she became famous.

One of the most expensive moments on TV for which I was responsible was a visual gag on Children's ITV: Cheryl Baker of Bucks Fizz fame was linking programmes while complaining about strange noises from the basement below the studio. For this script we had commissioned a special Basement set – full of complicated pipework, including a big hidden tank of green gunk that would pour over Cheryl on cue. We had recorded all that day's normal footage by half past five, giving us half an hour to set up and record this final funny scene. Failing to finish by six meant the studio hire costs would rise rapidly and the crew would start to claim overtime. Cheryl wanted to walk through the action and practice the dialogue. Good plan. Alas, she accidentally bumped the pipework above her head releasing the gunk which gushed to the floor, missing her and not being recorded because the cameras were not operating. To fulfil the day's script, we needed that slapstick scene, so I had to send most of the crew for a slap-up supper while the scene hands and I scooped up gallons of goo back into the tank. It took three hours and thousands of pounds to re-stage and film a ten second shot of Cheryl Baker being gunked - which didn't seem funny at all by the time we did it.

Scene 7   Library and Museum

On the corner of this handsome building we can see the date when it was officially opened by Mayoress Lady Mary Lygon. Where did the money come from? Profits from Worcester's hugely successful exhibition of 1882.

Many provincial cities and towns staged exhibitions through the 19th century, before and after the celebrated Hyde Park extravaganza of

1851. Worcester pulled in a mind-boggling array of objects made within the county – which at that time embraced much of Dudley and Halesowen. The event was staged in the vast railway engine workshop that still sits at Shrub Hill. Among the subjects on display were 'boot and glove making by machinery', '8 ton railway wagon wheels' and 'modern Worcestershire pottery and glass'. Fortuitously, the event was very well received by the national press. The Times considered it was 'more excellent than had hitherto been attempted in the provinces, Manchester, excepted'. Hence many visitors and an accumulation of cash. Thus the 1896 Victoria Institute, which later became the city's Library and Museum – as titled on the front of the building. Now, of course, it houses a delightful museum and art gallery.

I'm a bit of a buff on exhibitions having made a string of television programmes set within major British exhibitions. 'Gaz Top Non Stop' saw presenter Gareth Jones take a continuous journey through events such as the Earls Court

Boat Show, chatting to stand staff as he went, all captured on a single camera generally edging backwards as the never-lost-for-words host powered forward. Typically he would interview six people across seventeen minutes, to provide a finished one-third segment for an ITV one-hour slot with two commercial breaks - yet without any edits.

High-energy, fact-finding when roving reporter Gaz Top takes a non-stop tour of some of the world's biggest and brightest exhibitions and trade shows.

The programme we made in Worcestershire was at the final day of the Three Counties Show which was at that time primarily an agricultural event held across the middle of the week. We walked through all the stalls and marquees to negotiate a pleasing, viable, interesting route. Gareth and the camera crew arrived on day three once that trajectory was agreed.

To clarify the structure: opening credits, then a 17-minute long, single-camera moving-backwards shot of Gaz meeting and chatting to people on half-a dozen stands, then an End of Part One animated caption linking to the first commercial break. And so on, to make a low-cost, fast-action, vibrant, late-night factual hour. Daunting or what? I must have been mad.

Error of judgement

As we are close to a gallery, this seems a good time to enlighten art lovers about my alarmingly close encounter with a Picasso. I am in Hollywood, soon to interview the esteemed director of 'The Ghostbusters', Ivan Reitman. He is out to lunch and we have been told that we can set up our kit in his office ready for when he gets back. It's a huge office, as you would expect of a mighty film director with many credits and commercial successes to his name. There are desks and conference areas and lots of awards, props and fancy furniture in all directions, not to mention fine paintings on the walls, plus many more not yet hung.

The secretary told us we could set up wherever we liked. She had gone for lunch too. So our cameraman brought in his instrument and tripod, the sound man started to rig his mics and the lighting guy began deploying lamps around the area where we aimed to film. They needed no help from me so I took a photograph of the secretary's open log of Ivan's outgoing phone calls that morning. This included one to Arnold

Schwarzenegger ('WCB'). I have it to this day. But suddenly the glorious moments of luxury, leisure and media magic were shattered by a nasty rasping noise – which is what the leg of a lamp tripod makes when it slices through a Picasso painting that is leaning against the side of a sofa. The lighting man had had a little accident.

TV and film crews on location are covered by enormous levels of insurance against all eventualities. Our policy ran into millions, yet I immediately feared it would be insufficient to absorb the destruction of a Picasso. I knew my TV directing career had come to a horrible end. I was close to fainting when the secretary returned and I broke the news to her of our unforgivable stupidity and incompetence. She took one look at the Picasso and smiled. This was simply a prop from one of Ivan Reitman's films – 'Legal Eagles' – about art frauds, starring Robert Redford.

And so, shaking, we soberly continued our preparations.

Scene 8   Shire Hall

Queen Victoria enjoys an elevated view of the top end of Foregate Street from her pedestal within the frontage of this fine structure. Inside, the Worcester News can be sure of gathering copy most days. From the tragedies, explanations and excuses, your average reporter will be able to shape up some compelling paragraphs of sad and shocking human conditions.

Journalists are drawn to trouble. It's their bread and butter. I remember a news editor at Central TV explaining how his career had rocketed forward after he had been "lucky enough" to be the only person in the news room on a slow news day in Cardiff when the phone rang with a call from Aberfan: 'slag heap suffocates school children' – professional gold dust.

'The Antiques Roadshow' core personnel occupy a calm, civilized, open-plan office on Whiteladies Road in Bristol. But one quiet morning was abruptly interrupted when a BBC manager ran in and shouted across to the executive producer: "Jill Dando's been murdered. Can you dig out some footage of her for the lunchtime news". The room was occupied by a number of people who had been colleagues of Ms. Dando for many years. Not the best way to learn of a loss.

What's Jackson's encounter with crime, you ask. When responsible for 'Children's ITV' in

Birmingham I was obliged to entertain special guests who had come into the studios to talk about their latest show. One visitor was a "national treasure". I would take him for lunch to the Repertory Theatre across Broad Street. On the way, passers-by would wave and cheer, bus and van drivers would toot horns. He could do no wrong.

After our programming had been transmitted and the special guest had been escorted to his chauffeured car, one of the young women in our team came into my office, shaking, and told me to never leave her in the studio with that man again. After the crew had gone, she had been assaulted by the visitor. I asked her if she wanted me to make a formal complaint about the incident. She said No – it could be bad for her career.

And so the star could continue his furtive gropings with impunity. I find it impossible to believe that no one working on 'Top of the Pops' suspected Jimmy Savile of inappropriate behaviour in his dressing room.

A Blindfold Mile

The Justice Centre often has clusters of 'customers' hovering outside awaiting news of their case. The building has an overhang on its frontage, thus providing a small area of protection from any rain. So it was an ideal way-station for an elaborate mass walk through Worcester to promote the Sight Concern charity on a Saturday morning. The principle was that pairs of volunteers would walk through the city centre, with one party blindfolded and being led by the other – both people wearing branded T-shirts.

Previously Sight Concern's fund-raising events had taken place in discreet venues whereby sometimes very few people other than the participants knew what was going on.

In contrast, this project was designed to have thousands of people see the fifty couples edge their way along pavements and pedestrian areas – giving themselves and observers a sense of the challenges of dealing with sight loss.

The couples swopped roles at the way-points along the route, so both parties experienced the disconcerting nature of no visual references while moving through the middle of a busy city, and, alternatively, the need to carefully and diplomatically aid someone with visual impairment along pavements and around lamp-posts and other silent items of street furniture, either permanent or temporary.

The Blindfold Mile worked well and we were delighted that the Worcester News saw fit to give the event generous coverage across its pages at the start of the following week.

Medical matters

I have been privileged to act as the conduit in reaching troubled families for media projects. The BBC sent me to Glasgow to spend days and nights in the home of a man suffering from motor neurone disease. I captured his devoted family doing everything possible for his welfare. His wonderful wife Margaret broke down in tears when she showed me pictures of their wedding and the big, handsome, healthy man she had married.

As we walk the streets of this fine city, most of us seldom imagine that such activity is not possible for some citizens. The Worcestershire Association of Carers asked me to make a film that showed examples of their work and responsibilities. Two households live close to where we are now. Their domestic circumstances were tragic. One man had been looking after his severely ill, house-bound and voiceless wife for twenty-five years. He bravely agreed to be interviewed as he showed us the complex regime he had to follow to sustain his wife's chronically limited existence. His determination, courage and candidness enabled the Association to gain far greater understanding of, and thus support for, their vital services.

Wielding cameras in a medical environment is always a delicate and awkward matter requiring considerable diplomacy. Hereford's Rural Media Company hired me to film care home residents. One centre was keen to show the attention they paid to new residents entering with existing problematic conditions. A bed-bound old lady had been brought in and was having intensive treatment for her chronic bed-sores. It was decided that we should capture the necessary procedures.

The old lady agreed this should be done. I would need to focus the camera on her bottom. Best vantage point was above the bed, looking down, therefore the sound man and I rigged up a table that I could stand on at the end of the bed. He would hold his microphone boom at an angle to pick up the voices of the medical staff and the patient while I filmed the action.

We took up our positions and the procedure commenced. The old lady had her bedsheet pulled back, then she was turned over and had her nightie pulled up – to reveal a pus-ridden, bloody bottom. Somehow I manage to maintain a steady, in-focus shot of this gruesome mess - despite the ghastly groan and noisy crash as the sound man passed out.

I failed miserably to be professional during a visit to Great Ormond Street Children's Hospital. I was accompanying Matthew Kelly who, before the establishment of his greatly respected acting career, was a popular host of light entertainment programmes. I was so disturbed at the sight of tragic children looking dreadfully sickly I became unable to speak - choked up. Whereas Matthew brought his immense charm to every bed, chatting to everyone and clearly cheering the anguished parents. For this I will always hold Matthew in the highest regard.

Matthew was one of the presenters of London Weekend Television's peak-time prank show, 'Game for a Laugh' (along with Jeremy Beadle, Henry Kelly and Sarah Kennedy). Viewers did not see the results of every comic set-up, because in some cases the gag seriously backfired and the victims could not see the funny side. Instead they took legal action against the producers and generally achieved considerable financial settlements out of court - which required all parties to remain silent for ever more about what had happened in front of the cameras.

Directing on location

When I first started to work for the BBC towards the end of the 20th century, the Corporation was seeking to undertake a sea-change in its cultural profile, moving away from Oxbridge graduates dominating the on and off-screen Home Counties landscape - instead endeavouring to embrace and reflect the regions. Broadcast executives had learnt that people on Tyneside, in Glasgow and along the Welsh valleys don't like being told what to do by ex-public school boys. The biggest asset I brought as a location director to the Beeb was my regional accent.

Key location directing skill is communication – explaining to those around you precisely what you want in a way that convinces them it's the best thing to do. Rapidly establish rapport with those soon to be in front of the camera. Cause them to forget about the build-up of equipment around them and instead concentrate on their personal relationship with you. I once had to interview a cross-dresser. I spent a long time in his company before persuading him to put on his women's clothes and make-up. Once he was in front of the camera I told him he looked very good.

Never settle for the first option of a camera position. Consider left and right, up or down, or moving somewhere else altogether. Forensically study what lies in front of the lens. Could there be a smudge on the glass, dandruff on a collar, a distracting Coke can over a shoulder? If you are not looking through the view-finder yourself, demand a location monitor so you can see precisely what the camera person is recording. This is what the editor will face back at base. Examine that rectangle. Is there anything visible that would be better moved or removed? I made some episodes of a garage-sale-type show for ITV. Crowds gathered outside the house ready to explore the bargains beyond the gate. Vital shot was the residents cutting the ribbon to allow the punters to charge through. I called "Action!" but as the wife wielded her scissors the look on her face was, for a second, one of dismay rather than relish. No way of editing this moment out. I yelled "Cut!" and demanded everyone return to First Positions for a Second Take. I immediately took the woman to one side and congratulated her on what she had done so far and explained that a little camera problem had spoiled the ribbon-cutting shot so we would have to do it again. And wasn't this a marvellous moment in her family's story.

For these progammes the crew sometimes ran out of interested members of the public during the afternoon and so were short of film footage of negotiations and purchases of sale items. It has been claimed that passing school children were given cash to buy things from the garage, but I have no knowledge of this.

Camera crew or solo?

I am the proud owner of a fine Sony HDV Z1 instrument. My friends at Maverick TV were pioneers in having a director work alone with a handycam. This achieved access and intimacy with reserved individuals. However, to film with a camera-person and sound recordist allows you to concentrate entirely on framing, appearance, performance and dialogue. Doing everything yourself requires complete mastery of the gear and the ability to operate it while clearly concentrating on the person in front of the lens.

Scene 9   Puppetland

The stylish Ducati dealership was once an up-market burger bar, where one of the waitresses was a talented Canadian puppeteer. She helped me breathe life back into Scally, the big talking dog we had created for Children's ITV. She was great at doing his head, mouth, hands and tail, but struggled to supply his Liverpudlian accent.

Scally was born to outclass Phillip Schofield's pathetic BBC sock, Gopher. Our puppet was designed and built by a 'Spitting Image' regular, and operated by a team of two – one doing the head, mouth and voice, the other person arming the second hand and wagging tail. These two talented guys brought immense appeal to the cheeky animal. Then they fell out, and refused to work in the same studio. Their relationship had collapsed and thus their work ethic too. We suffered a series of clumsy outings for Scally who lost his smooth style and wit. Sometimes a floor manager or researcher had to operate a part of the furry creature from below the desk and we all knew this was a poor substitute for the real thing.

When Sir Lew Grade brought the Muppets to the UK, trenches had to be dug in the floor of an Elstree studio so the tall puppeteers could comfortably work standing up, while the puppets appeared at the height of the lenses of the pedestal cameras. When 'Spitting Image' set up in Birmingham, rather than destroy the studio floor, the cameras were raised to reach the eyeline of the foam Margaret Thatcher and her "vegetables".

For impressive manipulation of a puppet no-one could match Roland Rat's master, David Claridge. To deliver an interesting live TV segment, David would – in advance - photocopy a letter from a viewer and tape the copy to the underside of the desk where he would squat with headphones and a microphone fixed to him. Once on-air, viewers would see Roland holding the original letter in one hand, reading out a phone number, then picking up a phone and dialling that number in order to speak to the child who had sent in the letter – all amidst verbal interruptions from two other (puppet) characters in the wings. Think about the complexity of handling all these elements seamlessly whilst in character and crouched underneath a desk – conveying something impossible yet believable to four million kids.

On one occasion Roland made a hand puppet from some fabric, then operated this on his hand, to conduct a vigorous argument between the fabric puppet and the almost-human Rat. Amazing.

Puppetless

I worked with Rod Hull a number of times and found that, once he had put that unpredictable emu back in its case, he was an amiable fellow who enjoyed the ordinariness of life away from the limelight. A colleague of mine was tasked with producing a new series of the Rod Hull show for ITV. The format included a children's dancing sequence and, as you can imagine, there was much competition for those treasured roles.

The prime dancing schools were invited to offer forward anonymous candidates for consideration. My colleague, Phil, fixed a series of audition dates. Rod decided to attend. He explained that his daughter was among the candidates. Phil wanted to know the girl's name, but Rod wanted no favouritism in the process. The performers were to be chosen on merit alone. Of course, Phil knew it was essential Ms. Hull got picked. So he had the agonizing experience of sitting next to Rod watching each girl and trying to judge if she looked like Rod and so could be his daughter, while snatching glances at Rod to see if there was any flicker of acknowledgement between a father and his offspring. Rod then wanted to know Phil's views on each girl. There followed a painful dialogue as Phil tried to be non-committal about clumsy junior hoofers, fearing he was about to put his foot in it and describe the precious child as a no-hoper. Mercifully, as he pirouetted across emotive eggshells, Phil gleaned a sense of which auditionee was the star's blood relative and so was able to declare his eagerness to sign up the youngster - who Phil candidly estimated could well become the next Fonteyn.

Cutting edge

Back in the early 1970s I was immensely lucky to be given the opportunity to research a film about a new Gerry Anderson series, 'Space 1999'. Gerry had given the world many wonderful string-puppet science fiction shows, not least the iconic 'Thunderbirds'. But grown-ups could only take so much of strings poking out of people's heads – jet age folk who never walk anywhere but only move by some mechanical means - so it was decided to combine Gerry's capacity to create wonderful structures of the future with real actors in weird outfits delivering dramatic dialogue within mock-up moon modules.

The programmes would be made at Pinewood and Bray. Pinewood was where the actors worked. On the day I was allowed on set, there were teething troubles with the outer space automatic doors. As leading astronaut Martin Landau approached a door, it was meant to slide open with a barely audible hiss so his character could pass through that portal. In practice, the door was operated by a scene hand who tried to yank it to one side then shove back again. But the door was jamming against its runners and intensive carpentry was not producing a smooth motion. Instead the door clunked across, stopping halfway and causing the scene hand and the actor to issue expletives.

Over at Bray the model makers were busily shaping the landscape of the moon and its transport systems. In one studio a big convex surface five metres across was suspended in a steel frame. The surface was covered with small craters and I realised this represented a section of the moon. In the middle were some buildings the size of toy railway stations, but styled as futuristic space accommodation. Several modellers fiddled with the cute little structures, then the whole segment of lunar surface was cranked through 180 degrees to turn it upside-down. The camera was now pushed in to sit directly below the crafted buildings, pointing up toward them. We were told to stand back and put on goggles.

"Action!" The tiny moon station suddenly broke apart with a splutter of sparks and flames, all the bits dropping on to the camera lens. Gerry explained this was a cheap way of getting a big explosion. Every bit of the break-up of the model station accelerated - due to gravity - in the viewer's direction. Sound effects would confirm this had been an enormous eruption - as the script required.

Next door a major spaceship was under construction. It was four metres long but would look 300 metres once blended into the distant galaxy background. A modeller tipped bags of disposable razors out of a Boots the Chemist carrier bag on to his workbench. Why? The neat little handle of each razor would be cut and painted to represent one of the many massive steel girders holding the atomic engines of the extra-terrestrial ship to its superstructure. Try and catch an episode to see dozens of giant Gillette products gliding through the solar system, massive explosions hurling tons of debris in all directions and human beings striding through hissing doorways to discuss inter-planetary matters with a green-skinned person sporting plastic fins glued to her shaved head.

Good old Gerry.

Sports days

Worcester's great sports day is definitely the 10k run event that sets off from Croft Road below The Hive on a September Sunday.

Very little of my working experience has taken me near the world of sport. Closest was a film on the ex-England cricketer Gladstone Small. He arranged for us to bring a camera alongside the practice nets at Edgbaston so we could be a few feet away from hard ball hitting hard bat at international speed. Despite the net protecting us from any stroke or trajectory, the violent impact of those unforgiving surfaces was most alarming.

Years later I spent several months manipulating smaller balls around swanky golf clubs in the company of ex-Goodie Tim Brooke-Taylor to make fifteen new episodes of his Discovery series. Tim tolerated the crew telling him where to position his bag, where to stand, which way to face and when to hit the ball (multiple times from different camera angles) and when to walk – in the company of the local Pro, discussing golf and life and 'The Goodies' as they played.

Could we capture Tim's ball landing at some point on the fairway? Of course not. Tim was a very good golfer, but not so good as to be able to deliver a series of balls to the same spot. However, the club's Pro had the capacity to achieve such accuracy. So we would walk to the point where Tim's ball had stopped, aim the camera at it, then take Tim's ball away and ask the Pro to send an identical ball through the same arc to that location. Bingo.

After the final recording, we all went to a municipal course, hired sets of clubs and gave Tim a camera, so he could follow us around criticizing our efforts and mocking our behaviours.

Scene 10   The Hive

Worcester is immensely lucky to have its University which includes the excellent Hive library, archive and learning centre. Splash TV was lucky to be invited to make a film of the great opening event staged within the Hive – a promenade play conveying how the site had once been the city's cattle market. This was the work of Worcester's terrific Vamos Theatre – masked performers moving through the ground floor of the building, scene by scene, song by song. We used two cameras at a variety of different locations on three consecutive performances and crafted the six versions into one whole film.

Not long after this, we were asked to make a promotional film for the Worcestershire Local Enterprise Partnership. As you would expect, this required many meetings to contemplate possible content.

It was decided to include a shot of a long, twin-ended High Speed Train leaving Worcester and heading over the viaduct on its way to Hereford. The best camera location for such a shot was to access a top floor window in a nearby office block from where we could see the Hive building, then have the train emerge from the side of the Hive gathering speed while going westward over the river.

So we negotiated access to a suitable office and arranged on a sunny day to have its window opened. From Foregate Street station we were alerted by phone to the departure of the train. And so our cameraman captured a perfect shot as required for the film.

The project was almost complete when a member of the steering committee insisted the train would look better if coming from Hereford into Worcester, thus disappearing behind the Hive. But by now we had run out of time, budget and energy, so instead of organizing a re-shoot for this single element in the film, we simply reversed the existing shot. And thankfully, no-one ever complained to us that above the viaduct you could see birds flying backwards.

Within the Hive's library, on the third floor World War Two shelves, is a copy of Splash TV's film of testimony of military veterans of that conflict who were living in the county in 2013. Reading Max Hastings's brilliant 'All hell let loose' drove me to explore the possibility of finding and interviewing such people while they were still alive. Worcestershire County Council supported the project and managed to win funding from the Armed Forces Community Covenant.

WE DID OUR BIT

An 11 minute film featuring the accounts of 11 veterans who fought in World War Two and live in Worcestershire.

Hence, on 11th November of that year, an 11-minute DVD of their testimony was widely circulated to schools and other organisations, and screened inside the Hive itself.

We then produced a longer version of 'We did our bit' to allow each of the 11 veterans more time to explain their often-terrifying experiences. To underline the sense of ordinary, elderly citizens having done extraordinary things, we gathered shots of each person out in the community; for example, Gwen Thomas at Sainsburys and Ted Miles at a concert in Huntingdon Hall. An image of RAF engineer Ted Miles being interviewed formed the cover of the original DVD sleeve.

I was shocked at what Ted Miles told us. In 1943 he had been based at a Bomber Command airfield in Lincolnshire where he and colleagues prepared up to thirty Lancaster bombers to fly out each evening across the North Sea to drop ordnance on Germany or German-occupied territory. He revealed that of the thirty aircraft, typically twenty-nine would return by the morning. So each night "we had lost one aircraft and seven trained men". I subsequently read about those missions and felt ashamed to have gone through life unaware of such statistics. More than 55,000 volunteer airmen died during those attempts to overcome the Nazi regime.

I reckoned most books on RAF war-time endeavours concentrated too much on the Few Spitfire pilots who fought in 'The Battle of Britain', so I resolved to pen a narrative that covered the spectrum of aerial events across those six awful years to emphasise the complexity of flying through World War Two.

It took three years of wide reading (much undertaken within The Hive) and interviews, plus visits to universities and the major air history facilities in the UK to reach a point whereby I felt I had a reasonable lay-person's understanding of some of the relevant issues, technology, techniques, strategy and impact.

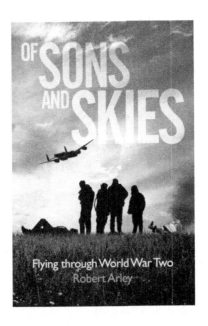

Sir Max Hastings very kindly allowed me to quote from his definitive titles in order to enrich my efforts.

One of the first people to buy a copy of the book directly from me was Lady Rosalind Morrison of Madresfield Court (President of Sight Concern). She later sent me a generous note of appreciation.

I have presented talks based on the book all over Worcestershire and beyond; perhaps most prestigiously at the Royal Aeronautical Society's Rolls-Royce branch in Derby in 2019.

Please note, I am always pleased to deliver an illustrated talk on this topic. See more on Page 102.

The Hive Archive holds the original production documents for the 'We did our bit' project, plus a hard drive of the full interviews with each veteran who contributed to this unique Worcestershire collection of WW2 testimony.

Scene 11   River Severn

And so at last to our city's mighty, magnificent river. Formed from Welsh rain, curving through Shropshire, the body of water that powers past our Cathedral is a formidable, defining force - at times muscular, at times benign, but unstoppable. It owns the plain and, when it wishes, will demonstrate its command of the landscape by cascading out across fields and properties to east or west of its route to the sea.

I have twice spent time on its banks with a camera gathering images of vigorous activity aboard water-borne craft.

For the Kidderminster Lions I made a film of their hilarious raft race from Arley (note that name) to Stourport – fancy-dressed folk frolicking above wobbly oil tanks and saturated pallets, commentary by Chris Barrie, AKA Rimmer from 'Red Dwarf'.

Then I tried to do justice to Worcester Rowing Club's precisely-structured Head of the River race – smart athletes articulating their delicate carriers on to the stream to cluster up at Bevere before executing machined strokes for a rapid, determined ride to beneath the city's bridges.

Several times a year the river reclaims its hinterland by seeping into parks and pubs, houses and pitches. Dutifully the BBC sends out an OB unit from Birmingham for the standard issue shot of the Severn plunging through the arches of the road bridge, the forlorn, flooded cricket club forming the backdrop. Here Nick Owen or one of his colleagues will explain the situation and exemplify the impact. They never tire of this task and we never tire of gasping at the audacity of mother nature to express her stunning status in our midst.

Blowing tops

Not everyone deals with fame and fortune the same. I remember overhearing a continuity presenter at ATV Studios in Birmingham explain to a colleague that she couldn't bear to go into Rackham's department store and not be recognised. Being fawned over by members of the public had become a drug for her. Being regularly on the telly turns a person from being an anonymous run-of-the-mill citizen to some sort of semi-public figure. Many on-camera people deal with it fine; but some have their sense of self-importance disturbed and distorted in alarming ways.

I was unsurprised to read of the bust-up in a hotel amongst a 'Top Gear' crew. After a long and demanding day on location, those presenters have reached a point whereby their perception of their value is at a heightened level, and thus their expectation of attention and support is hyper. Fury over poor service in a restaurant can blow into ugly rows very easily, and the crew – who also have had long, demanding days – can inadvertently say or do something that is interpreted by "the star" as insufficiently deferential or respectful. Bang.

I was on the receiving end of a blown top while directing an antiques programme. The presenter wanted to deliver a narrative about a First World War ship for which he had found an artefact on a table. He requested that the researcher find out more details of the vessel. She googled some data and gave me and the presenter a sheet of background info. We set up the camera in the middle of the auction house on the viewing day; people milling around considering prospective bids. When the presenter was ready we started to film him and his monologue, but within the first minute he incorrectly named the skipper of the vessel, and so I announced "Cut". And immediately the presenter blew his top. How dare I interrupt him when he was in full flow.

Many years of experience had taught me that there is no point in continuing with any piece-to-camera recording if the speaker has used an incorrect key name. I pointed out that he had wrongly named the skipper. We both had the same sheet of paper with the details; for some reason he had said a different name.

The presenter claimed that this minor discrepancy could have been "sorted out" in edit – by replacing the word with the correct name. But I knew that the presenter would need to refer to the skipper on multiple occasions and so the idea of "dropping in" a correction would never work. I was given a severe and loud dressing down in front of my crew and all the people in that room at the time. And because I was there as an agent of the BBC I could not abrasively respond to the utterly unjustified critique. Instead I apologised (through gritted teeth).

Scene 12 St Johns

Crossing the river takes us to the corner of Cripplegate Park, north of which on the Hylton Road we find the University's Arena, one of the country's finest stadia for basketball, both able-bodied and wheel-chair bound. Catch the latter to thrill at the capacity of world-class players shaping up for their next Olympic bid.

Beyond the Arena we reach the BBC Hereford and Worcester HQ, which I frequently visited to take part in "down the line" interviews with local radio stations situated by one of the motorways featured in my Motorway Guides.

Further on, we come to the University campus where Sight Concern staged an evening fund-raising fire-walk in the car park - yours truly to capture it. Health and safety issues positioned the event far from every building. Patently darkness was essential, so the car park lights were switched off - which meant my camera could see nothing but flames. So I had to hastily assemble a long, dodgy string of extension cables from the nearest three-pin plug to my single lamp close to the crowd – thus falling foul of all sorts of health and... yes!

The road westward at the side of Cripplegate soon becomes the A44 taking us to Bromyard where I once focused on a dozen Dads erecting home-made Christmas decorations for their High Street every autumn; Leominster where my camera encouraged a man with learning difficulties to reveal publicly the terrible bullying he had suffered as a child; then we reach the Dilwyn road-side lay-by where I persuaded a gypsy-traveller family to explain to BBC viewers their struggle to survive in a damp caravan, their parents having been welcomed at every local farm before mechanisation eliminated any need for their manual harvesting services.

South, we come to Malvern where I had to fight my way through a scrum of newspaper photographers to get a decent shot of the Duke of Gloucester unveiling Walenty Pytel's handsome buzzards sculpture.

Next, Ledbury where I managed to weave a gag into the opening of the Antiques Roadshow at its lovely market hall by revealing an approaching bus behind Michael Aspel, enabling him to describe the location as "Britain's most distinguished bus stop".

Then west to Hereford where my friend Kate Bliss neatly delivered a complex series of pieces-to-camera explaining and promoting drastic hair-cutting in order to support the admirable Little Princess Trust charity.

Scene 13   Cricket ground

I enjoyed an excellent balcony lunch here when good sport Philip Serrell invited some fellow workers to join him for a match overview.

Next year, for 'We did our bit' I brought army veteran Ron Hill to the terraces to watch a one-day game and gather angles to cover cuts in his narrative. This is an essential task within factual programme-making. Hardly anyone is able to speak for long without a fluff, error or long breath. Those breakfast TV presenters are exceptional. Seldom on location will an untrained individual be able to relate a single train of thought or neat story in one pleasing pass. Viewers don't want to see a series of jump cuts to the face of the speaker, so we acquire some suitable shots to "paste over" the necessary joins on the audio track.

Additionally, convention on mainstream TV is to have a shot change every three seconds. So if you plan to have an individual talk about something for a minute then the director needs to film at least twenty different shots of the subject matter in order to cover most of the useable minute with other complementary images.

I used to do some media teaching and often struggled to convince students that this formula of acquisition was essential to create a satisfactory end result.

Bridge changes Sunday night TV

Half-way along the south footpath of the city bridge is the ideal spot for an introductory image representing the city – the cathedral left of frame with the Severn and foliage to the right. Hence, in 1999, I brought Antiques Roadshow presenter Hugh Scully here to use this backdrop to film a piece-to-camera for the programme's opening.

As usual, he did a great job, but the requirement unsettled him, because he had visited this same spot many years previously doing more-or-less the same thing with a different director. And now he decided he had had enough - he had been round full circle.

Worcester had been one of his first Roadshows; now, more than a decade later, the city and thus location had come round again. Hugh elected to withdraw from the programme at the end of that season.

And so it was that through the following year I spent many happy days driving Michael Aspel around Britain, researching and recording Roadshow openings - all thanks to the view from the bridge.

Fame and fortune

After 'Monty Python's' Terry Jones escaped from the 'Flying Circus' he wrote some children's books. He came for a launch interview to our studio where I could not fail to notice he had a black eye. The day before he had been at the wheel of his swanky new BMW when he witnessed a collision between a van and a bicycle. Clearly the van driver had caused the crash so Terry pulled up alongside the resulting argument and, through his open window, shouted to the van driver that the incident had been that driver's fault. The angry van man was in no mood for observations from a rich toff so stomped towards Terry, who fumbled with the buttons for raising his window. Before the Python star could elevate the glass, van man punched him. Our make-up girl successfully disguised all evidence of the bruise for our cameras, and Terry chose to keep the make-up on to improve the rest of his day.

Bob Hope was contracted to host a 'Royal Variety Show' from the London Palladium one year. His team sent over scriptwriters from the States to draft topical gags that would play well with the British audience. On the day before the show, a rehearsal of all elements was staged. Only one person was missing – Tommy Cooper. Bob took this as an insult and reckoned Cooper should be dropped from the schedule. But the producers assured the American that all would be right on the night. Next evening the Royal party arrived and the show began. Still no sign of Tommy. Bob commenced his carefully crafted comedy – all copied on to large cue boards held up on both wings of the stage. While a dance troupe were re-enacting a West End musical number, Bob was told that Tommy had arrived. With disgust, Bob linked to Tommy who wandered on to the stage holding a battered suitcase and a card-table - to get far bigger laughs than Bob had achieved so far.

Andrew Davies, the celebrated adaptor of classical novels into TV fare, told me how his career took off. He was working at Warwick University and dabbling with scripts when offered a slot at Coventry's Belgrade studio theatre for a brief run of his new play about a troubled school-teacher. This achieved a positive two-paragraph review in The Guardian which caused Glenda Jackson (no relation) to request a copy of the script. She persuaded Andrew to make changes to the narrative that placed the teacher more strongly centre-stage. Within a few weeks Andrew supplied a revised version, and a few weeks later Ms. Jackson's manager announced that the play would open in the West End and that Andrew would receive the standard 7.5% of the weekly box office takings. Ten days after the play opened, Andrew got a cheque for £1,500 in the post. Seven days later, another envelope arrived containing a similar amount. This went on for months, then the play and Ms. Jackson transferred to Broadway. Now Andrew's weekly cheques were in the region of $2,500. He and his family did not know what to do with all that money. Six months later, Glenda re-joined her friends at the Royal Shakespeare Company to tread those hallowed boards once again on modest wages.

Before Benny Hill became branded as sexist, he made many shows at Teddington studios that achieved great ratings right around the world. The funny man lived on his own and would occasionally arrange to go to the home of his choreographer for a breakfast meeting. He would travel by bus with his script in a carrier bag. Libby would rustle him up a big cooked breakfast (which often seemed the whole point of the meeting). On one occasion she told Benny to note a phone number, so Benny pulled a small piece of paper from his shirt pocket and scribbled the number down. After Benny had finished his breakfast, sorry... meeting, he headed back to the bus stop, then Libby saw he had forgotten to take the phone number. She picked up the paper and unfolded it to discover Benny had written on the back of a cheque for over $200,000 – his latest royalty payments for sales of 'The Benny Hill Show' in the USA.

Scene 14   Browns

Our Media Mile comes to a halt by the fizzy, funny fountains adored by four-year-olds. In the adjacent car park I staged a scene with Henry Sandon for the film we made for the Royal Porcelain Museum. This area had been the site of an early porcelain factory, and when Henry first came to the city as a cathedral chorister he had spent lots of time digging for fragments of pottery, firstly in his own garden (by the Bishop's Palace), then here where - years before the tarmac was laid - he unearthed shards of Roman material as well as intriguing segments of 18th century plates and jugs.

Henry was on camera as a child. He and his family lived in Soho and Henry was given cheeky kid roles in early, short films being made on his doorstep. So when he eventually became the curator of the Museum, he had a great gift for mass communication. And thus he became a valued player in the Antiques Roadshow team, ultimately replacing Arthur Negus as the beloved grand old man of ancient artefacts. A further great strength he brought the Roadshow was his affable, enthusiastic manner with everyone. Some Roadshow experts were uneasy meeting ordinary people in the provinces, and tended to avoid unnecessary encounters with the masses unless an individual was offering some special object for consideration. Whereas Henry would walk along the queue before the doors had opened, chatting to everyone and making them feel special.

How fitting that one of the elements of the old porcelain factory which Worcester's TV star liked best – the original showroom – has been turned into a stylish arts centre and named The Henry Sandon Hall.

On the river path southward beyond the Cathedral we find the Kings School's distinctive boat house. I filmed a junior dance show in the Kings' theatre, staged by a smart teacher who always wore a bright red T-shirt to rehearsals. On show night she entered the auditorium and strode to the middle front row seat and took off her coat to reveal a lovely red dress that matched her T-shirt in colour. Co-incidence? No. The red was a beacon for the jumble of hoofing kids – a reference point for all their moves and performances. Clever.

Chris Tarrant was a student at Kings. Who knows if his subsequent media career is a selling point. Allow me to clear up a popular misunderstanding regarding the history of ITV children's programming. Chris was never an initial presenter of 'Tiswas'. He came on board after a few weeks as merely a last-minute replacement for a guest who failed to turn up. I had initiated what became Tiswas. I was a junior continuity script writer given the dull Saturday morning slots to fill. I devised competitions and other child-orientated elements which were pleasingly presented by novice continuity announcer Peter Tomlinson. This uncovered a large, previously untapped family audience and it was decided to mount a show specifically for that constituency.

Tiswas stood for "Today is Saturday, Watch and Smile". These days Chris travels rail lines with a camera crew while Peter is (at the time of writing) Chairman of Worcestershire County Council.

If you don't want a predictable career, television could be the route for you.

End credits

While in Los Angeles making the 'Real Ghostbusters' documentary I flicked through channels on my hotel TV and happened upon a truly horrible animation series based on the feature film 'Beetlejuice'. Like the movie, this was a world devoid of morality in which awful characters did nasty things all the time. It was a series without virtue and I was horrified that anyone had seen fit to produce such a thing.

Six months later I was even more horrified to learn that one of the Children's ITV controlling executives was proposing to screen the series here. The animations had been acquired as part of a package of American product and this man saw no reason not to include it in a future schedule. Up until now I had been a diligent, enthusiastic executor of the Children's ITV agenda. But I could not embrace this prospect which was utterly inappropriate for children's viewing. I challenged the decision and argued fiercely that the series should not be shown on our channel, making clear I would withdraw my company and our services from our contractual commitments if necessary.

The argument stayed under wraps. No-one blabbed to the press. The proposition split the steering committee and resulted in the ITV schedule being temporarily fragmented when some regions saw fit to run a few Beetlejuice animation episodes while others, including my home base Central TV, refused to screen the shows.

My contract was completed but not renewed. But here's the thing – most of the stories I have been able to tell across the previous pages have been because I then left the comfy, fabricated, fantasy environment within TV studios and instead worked out in the real world filming real people in real situations.

INDEX

My thanks to Michelle Doidge and the rest of the Worcester Tourist Office team for championing the Media Mile walks and this book.

And to Lisa Griffiths for designing the book cover and route map.

And to Gil Jackson and Peter Waldron for checking the text for legality.

[Nevertheless, in the event that you notice any reference which might be thought to be an inadvertent misrepresentation of a person or an organization, please bring this to our attention in order that we can assess whether it may be necessary to revise of some part of our well-intentioned text.]

BUY MIKE'S BOOK

FROM AMAZON

(Author's name appears
as Robert Arley, Mike's
writing pseudonym)

OF SONS AND SKIES

Fresh, accessible
exploration of the
terrifying challenges,
complexity and
consequences of WW2
aerial combat.

"Brilliant!"

"Fascinating!"

"A must read!"

Helps us appreciate
how lucky we are not to
have lived and served
through those violent
times.

ALSO ON AMAZON

Mike's previous book is set in Worcester - a teen comic novel, the cover image showing a scary moment when a miniaturised school girl encounters a hungry seagull outside the McDonalds near the river in St Johns.

BIG BIG SECRETS

Robert Arley

Want a arrange a MEDIA MILE WALK?

Go to worcestermediamile.com
Or call at the Worcester Tourist Office

Want to see clips of some of the films Mike mentions?
They can be found on YouTube. Search the YouTube
platform for: WORCESTER MEDIA MILE

Want to host a talk from Mike about his air war book?
Or find out more about Mike and his work?
Go to: www.robertarley.com

Printed in Great Britain
by Amazon